The Scientific Papers

The Leading Professor Miguel Angel Sanchez-Rey [*The Grandmaster*, *The Master of Space-Time*]

The Academy of Advance Science and the Technological Sciences

The Physicalist Program

Table of Contents

Anticipatory Shock in the Global Economy

Social democratic norms have kept world affairs relatively stable throughout the industrial and developing economies. Since then, with the collapse of the European Union and the permanent decline of the religious state, higher yields in inflation implies that demand is relatively stable.

But with deflationary policies, and a trade dispute across the other side of the pacific, purchasing power has begun to fall -- with increasing demand becoming more ominous. Meaning that higher prices makes purchasing power of goods and services inadequate. Such that New Keynesian policies, with the declining state and government sector, becomes inadequate in restoring purchasing power to sustain a growing world-wide economy.

With the breakup of the European Union, the beginning of
the corporate governorship in the U.S., the breakdown in the
Common Wealth of Nations, and the wide-spread panic of the
Commons (that has led to a growing immigration crisis on U.S.
soil) means the permanent demise of social democratic norms
and the toppling of New Keynesian economic policy.

Implies that the only way out is to *fully abandon the
international norm and to adopt the internationalist model* (for
the preservation of necessary economic policy that mandates
economic development and interdependence). Preserving what
remains of the central banks -- in order, to justify federalist
policies and free-trade agreements, that are essential for
continual global economic growth. Either way, lasting damage
has been inflicted to social democracy.

On Strange and Uncertain Times

At the *New York Times*, with very little prospect, the scientific propaganda machines are on the frontlines justifying and defending the centrist and right-wing political establishment. Producing all sorts of propaganda editorials to justify needless policy proposals in hopes of making pointless policy-making. Yet at the other end in, *The Guardian*, the U.K. establishment is overwhelmed with massive tax-cuts and state-sector privatization that has compromised its ability for non-partiality in editorial decision-making. Only encouraging the Tory-government to continue to incite British neo-Fascism and the solidification of the Brexit. At *Al Jazeera*, panic has surmounted with the U.S. withdrawal from the Iranian nuclear deal and the continuing regional instability of Palestine and/or Israel.

At a global stage, the strange and uncertain times of the current era is indicative of a modern dystopia in the Scientific Age. Where the tragedy of philosophical transcendentalism has cause the public sphere to fall victim to an ominous psychotic state. Whereby the radicalization of sciences has led to the complete radicalism of the political sciences. A mixture that puts an end to the dominance of the Western tradition of neo-liberal praxis.

What appears to be a vibrant political democratic movement to supplant the far-right establishment in the U.S., is instead a wishful dream to surpass the corporate-state sector -- when the beginning of the corporate governorship has meant the corporate takeover of state-industry and polity; especially the left-wing propaganda machines of the Western democratic countries.

That is, neither political movements (whether Democratic and Tea-party or even Tory and New Labor) will be able to fathom the depth of the radicalism of the public sphere (induce by almost 40 years of far-right economic policy) that evidently led to the breakup of social democratic norms -- in the form of an anticipatory aftershock, cause by the crippling trade dispute between the Chinese and U.S. government. Exacerbating political radicalism amongst the party establishment -- both in the United States and the United Kingdom.

These are strange and uncertain times, is very much true. But most importantly, fraudulent policy decision-making is nevertheless the nature of this profoundly strange and uncertain statement of political desperation to invigorate a failed policy era of cult-decision making.

Either way, the public sphere is too radically motivated to even consider heeding the political establishment (and their desire to uphold centrist policies and neo-liberal economics). Instead the public sphere is much more open to any form of political activism that leads to the realization of self-interests -- formulating itself as political and/or economic ideology that is utilitarian in construct.

With that in mind, not all things are what they seem. To look closely at the conundrum of propaganda machines and political and/or economic ideology, only exposes the core failure of pointless policy-making and needless policy proposals -- the careless nature of the scientific propaganda machine. A machine which is antithetically oppose to both global economic democracy and decision-making that is inherently democratic.

A conundrum to be wary of in a modernist dystopian

reality.

Political Authoritarianism

Political authoritarianism is a crime -- that much is said. But also an indirect consequentiality of the permanent decline of the religious state. For the limited state (or libertarianism), whether socialist and/or capitalist, is an unfathomable dream.

A dream which lurks in the very cognitive psyche of human inclination. And that the rise of authoritarian policies is a response to the growing force of hostility against liberal politics (that stresses inalienable rights and social democracy) and the threat of pure anarchism.

Within the modern world, authoritarian practices are imposed to protect the populace from pathological decision-making that could destabilize what remains of democracy and social tranquility. And that free association is not conducive for sustaining productivity at the expense of a disciplined democratic workforce.

    The general population does not revolt against the declining nation-state on the grounds of pure anarchist reasoning. For such reasoning argues for the attainment of a social democratic state base on libertarianism. But because social democracy has undergone an anticipatory shock, a democratic socialist state is the pipe dream of varying self-interest.

And that varying self-interest makes social

democracy -- of state-capitalism, an unlikely alternative to

state-industry and free trade. For the superstate is to be

quietly dismantled and what remains is Anarcho-

syndicalism.

And that authoritarianism is a counter-reaction to the

threat of nationalist sentimentality.

Anarcho-syndicalism is in the long-term. Instead

what lies beneath Anarcho-syndicalism is the inevitable

outcome -- a federation of democratic industries. And

that while others envision a differing belief in the

outcome of history, differing outcomes is an act of hasty anticipation.

And that the inevitable outcome is a crime to be reckon with and that the inevitable byproduct is a harsher reality (Anarcho-syndicalism is not a celebratory act but a cognizant problematic of radicalists political theory).

While countries pursue authoritative action to protect what's left of the religious state, there can be no tolerability of pure anarchism. And yet as nations hold strongly to federalism, there is little to be said about inalienable rights that infringe upon the commons. For inalienable rights are an inexactitude -- instead, self-management and self-actualization (through equal outcome) is the proper preference to the utilitarianism of the minimal state.

And that as political entities are inclined to the libertarian mind-set, and as nation-states implement authoritative action to protect what's left of the religious state, giving inceptives to the general population (in order to cooperate with the superstate) means the pacification of the individual.

As individuals undergo pacification, peaceful co-existence means a democratic federation -- govern by the self-management of the workers control of production and

the dominion of the superstate, until an economic

democratic federation replaces the borderlines of the

diminishing nation-state into regional sectors. And that

the council of the superstate take authoritative action to

protect the workforce (abolishing any opposition and/or

threat to the democratic order).

Utilizing authoritarian practices that pacifies the

population rather than by applying brutality and/or

resorting to the politics of terror.

A transgression -- in itself, but a necessary stipulation

for a healthy transitional period at the dawn of the

Advance Age. No other stipulation is adequate enough to meet such circumstances.

A revolt against the superstate is to be avoided at all cost. For there is no other alternative to Anarcho-syndicalism. Political authoritarianism is not to be misconstrued. There is a defining difference between political authoritarianism and authoritarian practices (implemented to protect and uphold the dominion of the superstate).

But the superstate is not the desired outcome. Rather the desired outcome is the blossoming of political anarchism -- yet a crime to be distrustful of.

The Fields Medal and the Prize System

The Scientific Age has unveiled a planet which has falling over the cliff. With the International Congress of Mathematicians announcement of the 2018 Fields Medal, it has occurred to many that the prize system has turn to cruel tactics to invigorate a shatter self-image. A shatter self-image that is a product of an era when prizes were awarded to the most substantial and significant academics and peace-keepers. Prizes that were meant to solidify globalist cohesion and to unite nation-states -- in what seem at the time, as a noble cause for self-actualization and world-fame.

But due to the information age, at the dawn of the Windows XP revolution, much of the general publics' notion of fame and fortune, i.e., academic and political success, began to fall apart. With prizes awarded to distinguish groups and individuals base on long-term political, corporate and/or strategic interest.

(Giving massive popular support for laureates and awardees that eventually prove inadequately incapable of confronting a modernist dystopian reality. As the prize system [which is far more brutal in comparison than the private sector] sought to award prizes [and money] to institutions, scientific, social and political figures on those long-term interest).

Yet those long-term interest can come into conflict in the short-term. With the 2007 Nobel Peace Prize (awarded to Al Gore and the United Nations Intergovernmental Panel on Climate Change), came the disastrous turning point when the 2015 United Nations Climate Change Conference, on global warming, did not agree to a binding agreement. Or that the 2014 Nobel Peace Prize led to the disastrous outcome of the Arab spring when sabotage became the deadly norm of the prize system.

Whenever prizes are awarded to high-stakes tasks and/or endeavors, does sabotage become a likelier prospect in the long-term (even the former president Barack Obama's Nobel Peace Prize in 2009 amounted to a failed policy era).

The Fields Medal has faired bitterly about the dystopian uniqueness of a once cohesive planet that is now more divided than before the Second World War. When Jewish science was coined to stigmatize the contributions of Jewish ethnic groups from the prize system (and much of the scientific academies and the learn societies of then divided European continent of the modernist age).

But yet self-actualization -- before the advent of classical globalization, was understood as a self-driven endeavor (even amongst mathematicians and like very much today, philosophers of many walks of life).

When lives are at stake, the top-prize is of little concern. When the future outcome of every living animal and abiotic life is at stake, distinguish prizes are just a short-live byproduct of brain euphoria and psychological narcissism.

One does not marvel at a prize or a collection of prizes, when one's life runs the risk of catastrophe. When the right thing to do is to avoid catastrophe and to abandon the prize (than to marvel at a dead or a hundred carcasses). The essence of the military chain of command -- even amongst the PHPR top-scientists.

For that matter, The Physicalist Program [PHPR] is *off-limits to the prize system* in the long-term.

The Academy of Advance Science and the Technological Sciences [AASTS] is a global scientific academy of higher learning -- meant to produce higher qualifications of world-leadership and renowned expertise, by taking leadership position.